Roll, Wheels, Roll!

Written by Meish Goldish

CELEBRATION PRESS
Pearson Learning Group

Wheels roll Sandy's seat.

Wheels roll under feet.

Wheels roll on a road.

Wheels roll a wide load.

Wheels roll on a rail.

Wheels roll a bag of mail.

Things With Wheels

 wheelchair

 in-line skates

 **car**

 **truck**

 **train**

 mail bag

What wheels do you roll on?